A Gift

For:

From:

Other Books by Bradley Trevor Greive

The Blue Day Book

Dear Mom

Looking for Mr. Right

The Meaning of Life

The Incredible Truth About Mothers

Tomorrow

The Book for People Who Do Too Much

Friends to the End

Dear Dad

The Simple Truth About Love

BRADLEY TREVOR GREIVE

BOK4309

Andrews McMeel
Publishing

This edition published in 2005 by Andrews McMeel Publishing exclusively for Hallmark Cards, Inc.

www.hallmark.com

ISBN: 0-7407-5822-5

Book design by Holly Camerlinck

Photo Credits

Acclaim Images (USA) • www.acclaimimages.com
Africa Imagery (South Africa) • www.africaimagery.co.za
Alamy Images (UK) • www.alamy.com
Australian Picture Library (Australia) • www.australianpicturelibrary.com.au
Austral International (Australia) • www.australphoto.com.au
Fairfaxphotos (Australia) • www.fairfaxphotos.com
Frans Lanting Photography (USA) • www.lanting.com
Getty Images (Australia) • www.gettyimages.com
Natural Exposures Inc. • www.naturalexposures.com
Pavel German Wildlife Images (Australia) • www.australiannature.com
Photography E-biz (Australia) • www.photographyebiz.com.au
Photolibrary.com (Australia) • www.photolibrary.com
PhotoNatureNet (Germany) • www.photonaturenet.com
Richard du Toit (South Africa) • rdutoit@iafrica.com
Ron Kimball Studios (USA) • www.ronkimballstock.com
Stock Photos (Australia) • www.stockphotos.com.au
Wildlight Photo Agency (Australia) • www.wildlight.com.au

Detailed page credits for the remarkable photographers whose work appears in *The Simple Truth About Love* and other books by Bradley Trevor Greive are freely available at www.btgstudios.com.

For Princess Panda
how I love you so.

ACKNOWLEDGMENTS

If ever I felt like a pungent fraud, this book proves that such inklings were perfectly correct. Like most men with an Australian passport, I have always been romantically dislocated, and thus would never claim to offer any significant insights pertaining to matters of the heart. All I know for certain is that before I found (or, depending on your point of view, was found by) My Beloved, I often felt curiously empty, a hollow peanut husk, a pie that was all crust. I now know that the emotional journey from lonely to loved is worthy of investigative contemplation, however flawed that may be. While creating the text of this book, I clarified a number of my most complex feelings and reexamined some humiliating episodes and twisted perceptions that I hope will connect with and amuse you, dear reader.

Writing this book was, as always, great fun. I offer eternal thanks to my publishers who, for better or for worse, encourage me to do what I love every day. I must make special mention of Christine Schillig, my manuscript midwife at Andrews McMeel Publishing (USA/UK), who flew all the way from Kansas City, Missouri, to Sydney, Australia, to help bring this little book into the world.

Without the stunning photographs contained in *The Simple Truth About Love* and the entire Blue Day Book series, the books would be a supremely underwhelming reading experience. Needless to say, I am very grateful to the hundreds of contributing photographers, and I encourage anyone interested in working with them or the photo libraries that have added so much to my work to seek out their updated contact details posted at www.btgstudios.com.

I owe the greatest debt to my literary agent and certified love god, Sir Albert J. Zuckerman of Writers House, New York. On numerous occasions, I have awakened Sir Albert in the middle of night to beg a salve for my tormented heart. After gently reminding me of the ten-hour time difference between Sydney and New York, Al often shared moving experiences from the Writer's Halfway House, a sanctuary for wayward authors he established in the Florida Keys.

The Writer's Halfway House was an unashamedly exclusive haven, and those without a rich publishing pedigree had to first prove themselves by arm-wrestling with Philip Roth—best of three matches. This trial eventually ceased after Roth fractured both of Charles Bukowski's elbows, an event Saul Bellow described as, "Blankly brutal, yet viscerally amusing," with Stephen King noting, "Whoa—so macabre!"

Al told me that most patients were simply lovesick. Their unrealized passions had fermented and turned their great romantic souls sour. Others had their fragile hearts shattered by lovers, critics, or both, and their platinum pens were paralyzed by pain. Too brilliant to suffer regular therapists and not physically robust enough to join the French Foreign Legion, the writers withered away in frustration.

Al's innovative regimen, focused compassionately on both mind and body, saved a raft of Nobel laureates. Generally speaking, deprivation was discouraged, and shock therapy was an optional extra. Instead, the treatment revolved around wholesome and varied creative stimulation that empowered each writer to rediscover his or her unique vitality and sense of wonder as a human being. Starting with nature walks, tiddly-winks, and macaroni pictures, broken authors and poets gradually increased their level of engagement with the intellectual, emotional, creative, and physical worlds. In addition to a series of informal seminars, water polo on pool ponies was always popular, as was the weight room, though the fully equipped boxing gymnasium was seldom used because Norman Mailer was always in there hugging the heavy bag, droning on and on about the "sweet science" till his listeners were out for the count. Still, it was amazing to watch invigorated Booker and Pulitzer Prize winners excitedly arguing the merits of their work on the sundeck while comparing their buff "six packs."

Not everyone enjoyed instant success. For many months, Ken Follett merely retreated to religion, going so far as to secretly replace his mattress with rough-hewn stones from Salisbury Cathedral. Hunter S. Thompson, considered by many a gate-crashing impostor, climbed out of a restroom window immediately after admission, only to sneak back inside every night to raid the dispensary. Sooner or later though, everyone, including these two gentlemen of letters, saw the light and was better for it.

To Al's eternal embarrassment, the Writer's Halfway House was closed by wildlife conservation groups in 1989 when, after leading a heated evening discussion about *The Naked and the Dead,* Norman Mailer strangled a raccoon in his sleep. Fortunately, by that time Al and his wife, Claire, had already rehabilitated many of the greatest writers of our time.

The secret of his success rate was surprisingly simple. "BTG," Al croaked wearily at 3:00 a.m. one morning, "all you have to do to prepare your heart for love is to let yourself fall in love with life itself. Love is the greatest inspiration for a writer—for anybody, for everybody. You cannot live without it. So celebrate love in all its forms, and it will never leave you. Celebrate life every day, and you will always live it to the full."

Sir Albert, I thank you from the bottom of my now considerably warmer and far larger heart.

Bradley Trevor Greive is the *New York Times* best-selling author of the modern classic *The Blue Day Book* and is a household name in thirty-five countries. His ten previous books have won awards worldwide and sold more than twelve million copies. Born in Australia, Bradley spent most of his childhood living in the United Kingdom, Hong Kong, and Singapore. A graduate of Australia's Royal Military College, he served as a paratroop platoon commander before leaving the army to pursue more creative misadventures. Also an award-winning artist, cartoonist, poet, toy designer, screenwriter, inventor, and qualified cosmonaut, Bradley lives mostly in Sydney, Australia.

The Anatomy of a Kiss

The fundamental facial mechanics of a kiss are
very well-known. Indeed, today the preparatory "pucker"
is universally accepted.

More than one trillion kisses have been successfully, or at least somewhat successfully, performed using this simple technique. Amazingly, no two kisses are exactly alike. Ever.

The intensity of kissing ranges
from a peck on the cheek

to the long, wet, passionate,
slightly sideways kiss on the lips, and, finally,

"Hello Mr. Tongue!"

The reactions from both parties at the conclusion are another variable of note. These can be an uncomfortable and unspoken "What the heck was all that about?"

Or, ideally, a violent post-smooch rapture

that leaves you tingling with goose pimples, feeling as if every atom of your conscious being is inflated with helium and you are in danger of floating off into the stratosphere.

In case you are wondering, this little book is about the love
that inspires such kisses—a love that sends your heart
soaring from here to eternity.

The Simple Truth
About Love

Falling in love is just like kissing—
no two people do it the same way.

A legendary romance may begin with the briefest
of beautiful encounters

or a casual introduction by a mutual friend,
who is then completely forgotten in all the excitement.

You might feel the hairs on the back of your neck stand up
as you turn to meet the piercing gaze of an enchanting stranger
across a crowded room,

across a parking lot,

a bowling alley,

or an all-you-can-eat-buffet.
The location really isn't all that important.

Often you are just sitting there minding your own business 9

and then *Wham!* Love suddenly hits you out of the blue,
and your pulse is off and running.

That such a fleeting chance encounter can result
in so many overwhelming feelings tells us a lot
about the power of love.

Like the sun or a fiendishly expensive designer fragrance,
love is an intoxicating force that draws all living creatures

(except for telephone salespeople who call you at home
and maybe aphids—we don't know about them for sure). 13

Love inspires us to do great, beautiful, terrible things
and a bunch of weird and stupid stuff

(all of which, curiously enough, can be found in Country
and Western music).

That's because when we fall in love, our reason
and perspective become distorted,

and we discover the lovers' paradox. Suddenly, we have
clear purpose, but we suffer overwhelming indecision. 17

The affectionate attention we receive means we feel
more self-affirmed and radiant than ever before,

and yet we are sick with self-doubt and insecurity.

Personal grooming also takes on a fresh energy,

sometimes to the point where we change virtually
everything about our appearance that turned our
admirer's head in the first place.

Though it is wonderful in so many ways, falling in love
can be a very unsettling experience.

Poetic torment churns in your soul
and keeps you from sleeping.

Whenever you close your eyes, the object of your desire
floats across a dreamscape toward your waiting lips.

In fact, the only time we really wake up to reality
is when the new lover is actually approaching.

Unfortunately, at that exact moment
your molecular structure turns to water.

You try to stay calm and composed, endeavoring to present a picture of charisma and confidence.

You fail.

All those breathless secrets in your heart that you rehearsed
a thousand times and are now ready to share gently
with a tender ear,

you suddenly blurt out, sounding like a race caller
from an ancient civilization.

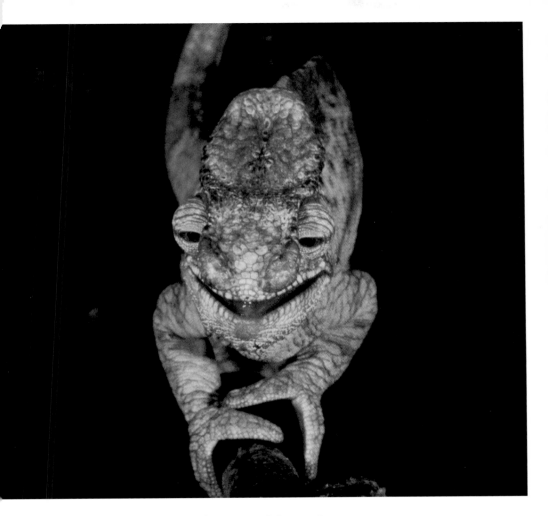

The key word is *patience*.

From a purely mathematical point of view,
with billions of people on the planet,
the romantic numbers are always on your side.

There is definitely someone out there
who is perfect for each of us,

so it makes no sense to grab the first cute butt
that walks by.

Don't be afraid to slow things down.

Really think about your feelings.
Run through a few emotional scenarios in your mind
and see how they look and feel.

There's a reason we feel so shy
when we first meet someone special.

Both people are seriously checking each other out,
looking for and revealing some very personal information.

The process is all about trust. Slowly, we get closer and closer.
Some things just shouldn't be rushed, and love is
always worth waiting for.

In its early stages, love is beyond wonderful.
Each moment together feels like a passionate embrace
in a magic forest.

You gallop tirelessly in perpetual and blessed sunshine,
your feet a few inches above the ground.

In other words, our perceptions of ourselves and our beloved
can become a touch idealized, to say the least.

We tend to forget that *Romeo and Juliet* did not,
in actual fact, end all that well.

The truth is that love is always beautiful,
and it may even feel perfect. But it can never be so,
not all the time.

Falling in love is an exquisite but complex
coming together of two individuals,

and a beautiful, dynamic relationship always has
some ups and downs. Imagine crossing an emotional ballet
with a washing machine.

The irritating thing about falling in love is that you don't suddenly get transported to the mythical Kingdom of Coupledom, where everything is designed to make your relationship perfect.

Two independently minded people usually have similar
but always slightly different needs,

and these differences keep us on our toes.
Surprises keep your love exciting and fresh,

but sometimes it seems as if you both
came from different planets.

One person is up when the other is down.

One wants to canoodle; the other wants to be left alone.

Even the most loving couples can't possibly agree
on absolutely everything. Take a simple misunderstanding,
combine it with a little poor communication,

then add some emotional baggage
from previous relationships,

and the romance starts to flounder.
A civil conversation can break down because of
a few careless or caustic remarks.

The salvo is then returned with interest,

and *Ka-Boom!* Open hostilities are declared.

Sometimes the dark, angry cloud evaporates as quickly as it built up, and all is forgiven and forgotten.

And sometimes it doesn't.

In which case, heartache is a certainty,

and, tragically, two people who seemed so right for each other
see all their hopes and dreams disappear.

And yet, if they would just make a little effort to reach out and reconnect, everything might be all right.

You'd be amazed at how quickly a quiet apology,
in word or in deed,

can return lost smiles to everyone.

The bottom line is that love, like everything else in life
that really matters, requires genuine effort.
Cuddles and kisses go a long way toward making love last,
but they aren't enough by themselves.

Sometimes, you have to get out and push
if you want your love to keep going forward,

which is why falling in love can occasionally be
almost as exhausting as it is invigorating.

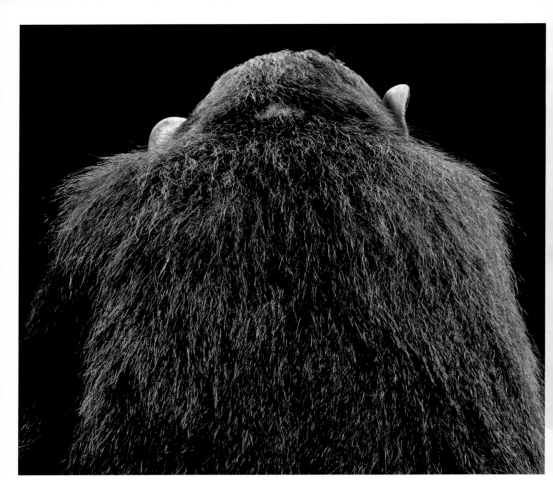

This is one of the two main reasons
some people turn their backs on love.

It's hard enough taking responsibility for your own feelings,
let alone looking after someone else's heart as well, right?

"Bah!" you say with false bravado. "Who needs all that schmaltzy love stuff anyway?" Which brings us to the second and most important reason people give up on love: Fear.

Fear of being hurt, fear of rejection, fear of potential lovers
who turn out to be evil people who take all the blankets
during the night and squeeze the toothpaste from the middle.
Fear is the number-one obstacle to falling in love.

But a little fear is not so terrible. In fact, it's normal and healthy.
No one likes to be naked and exposed or have their
dirty laundry hanging out in public.

Of course, much of this depends on whom
we are trying to get close to. A lot of people
are great but not great together.

If you can't have a difference of opinion
without getting your head bitten off,

if you are constantly being criticized

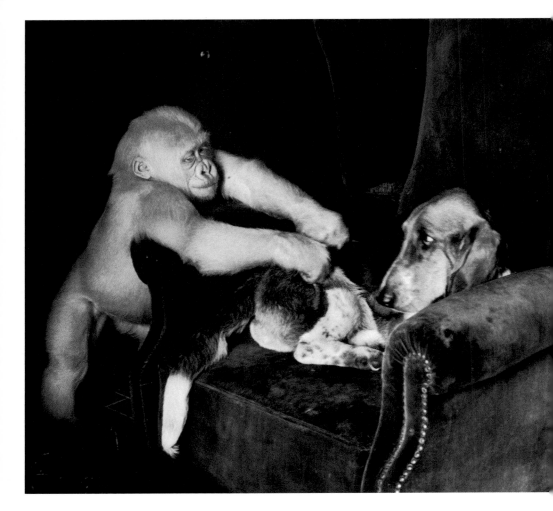

or bullied,

then maybe, just maybe, this isn't a perfect match at all.

In fact, you should probably get the hell out of there
while your heart is still in one piece.

While you're licking your wounds, you might also acknowledge your own part in the whole sorry mess.

Twenty-twenty hindsight can have tremendous value
if you accept the hard-won wisdom and move on
with life and love.

The journey to true love is not as daunting as it seems.

You don't have to lose yourself to find someone else.
On the contrary, different points of view are every bit
as important as the things you have in common.

Two lives. One love.

Your own personality flourishes in a relationship,

which brings out your best at home and at work.

Falling in love means you still get to do everything
that made you truly happy,

but now you also have the joy of sharing those things
with someone else. Plus, you get a whole bunch
of bonus benefits as well.

There are the quiet moments where boundaries dissolve
into a delicious all-encompassing oneness,

and there's the peace of mind that comes from knowing
that someone is there for you whenever for whatever.

There are great conversations about everything and nothing.

You can discuss your dreams and desires and know it is safe
to share things you could never say to anyone else.

When you are in love, there is snuggling,

explosions of passion,

and spooning, which, as scientific research shows,
makes your dreams twice as nice.

When you are in love, it means there is always someone
who will jump around with celebratory squeals
when you are a winner,

or give warmth and support when you are not.

Love gives us the strength to test the boundaries of our
weakness, knowing that when we get in over our heads,

a rescue mission is already on the way.

To experience such a relationship is to know
that every breath affirms that you are loved and that
true love overcomes all obstacles.

True love can climb the highest mountain
and cross the deepest sea

. . . eventually.

Love can endure the phone ringing in the middle of dinner

and survive numerous household accidents.

It can overcome debilitating back pain

and maybe even gallstones.

Love can overcome ludicrous working hours
and irritating Muzak while you're on hold.

Love overcomes abrasive in-laws,

chronic dandruff,

a visit from Mr. Sulky Pants,

and even episodes of insanity.
In other words, nothing can hold love back.
True love overcomes anything and everything.

Realizing the power of love feels like a light switch
is suddenly turned on inside your heart.

The world looks different.
Or perhaps you are looking at it differently.

Your search draws to a close.

You have finally found true love,

or true love has finally found you.

"Hello!"

~~THE END~~

The beginning